A CROWNING GLORY

St Helen's Church, the Great Hospital

A Crowning Glory:

the vaulted bosses in the chantry chapel of St Helen's, the Great Hospital, Norwich

by Martial Rose

Photography by Bruce Benedict

Larks Press

Published by the Larks Press
Ordnance Farmhouse, Guist Bottom,
Dereham, NR20 5PF
01328 829207

Website: www.booksatlarkspress.co.uk

Also published by the Larks Press

The Misericords of Norwich Cathedral
by Martial Rose and Ken Harvey

Except where otherwise stated, all photographs are by Bruce Benedict.

No part of the text or photographs in this book may be reproduced in any form without the permission of the author and the authorities at St Helen's Church, the Great Hospital, Norwich.

British Library Cataloguing-in-Publication Data
A catalogue record for this book is available from the British Library.

© Text: Martial Rose, 2006. Photographs: Bruce Benedict and Elizabeth Armstrong, 2006.

ISBN 1 904006 32 9

Acknowledgements

Many years ago trustees of The Great Hospital suggested that I should write a book describing the roof bosses in St Helen's chantry chapel, but it was Granville Holden's more recent work on such a project that prompted a more determined study of this subject. Granville Holden, a resident of the Great Hospital, died before his project had been completed. But friends and fellow residents at the Great Hospital completed his work and printed a few copies of a most attractive booklet which became the starting point for this present work. I should like to thank Alan and Rosemary Anderson for bringing Granville Holden's pioneering work to fruition.

My thanks are due to Mrs Dorothy North, The Master of The Great Hospital, for allowing me to undertake this study and for her support in providing me with unpublished papers concerning the history and structure of St Helen's church. I have been greatly helped by the interest and enthusiasm of the Reverend Madeline Light, the Chaplain of The Great Hospital, and by Barbara Miller. Publication of this work has been made possible through the generous support of the Greene Charitable Settlement, the Scarfe Charitable Trust, Joan Martin, and the Trustees of The Great Hospital.

Elizabeth Armstrong has encouraged me in this undertaking and has been supportive at every stage. There is no measuring my indebtedness to her. Some photography has been undertaken by Elizabeth Armstrong, Cameron Benedict and Jenny Rose, but by far the largest contribution has been made by Bruce Benedict, often precariously perched on a moveable platform in the chantry chapel. Bruce Benedict's work will show more eloquently than my text that these carvings have been executed by a master craftsman. But it is the skill of another master craftsman, the photographer himself, that has made such images and their analogues so readily available to us.

Plan of the Bosses
as seen looking up

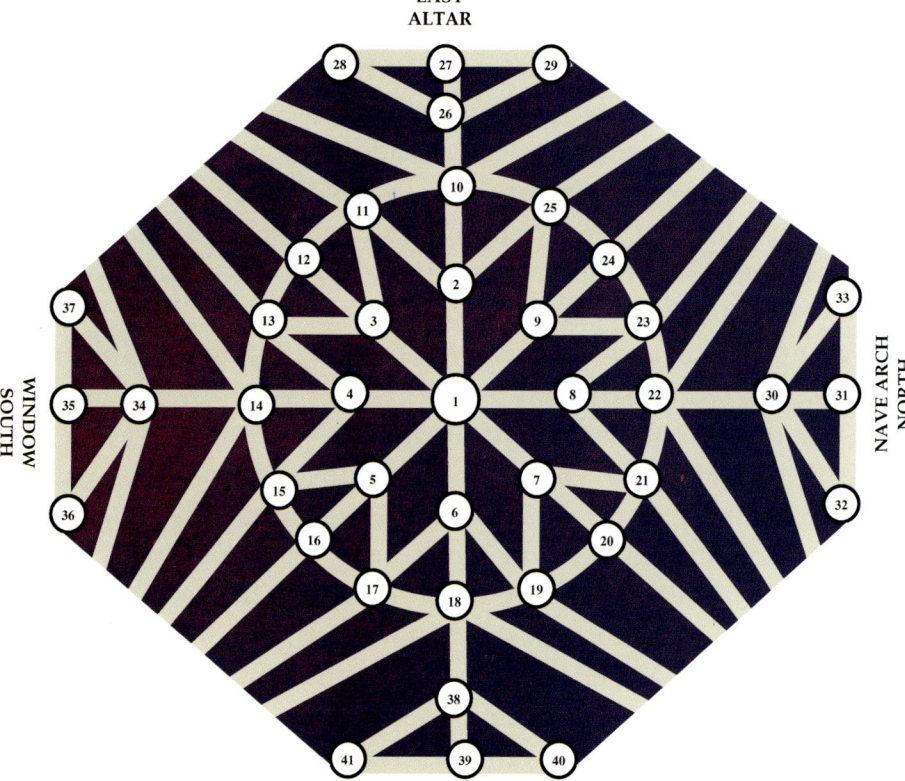

Central	1	The Coronation of the Virgin Mary			
Inner Circle	2	The Nativity		6	The Ascension of Christ
	3	Saint Edmund		7	Saint Edward
	4	The Resurrection of Christ		8	The Annunciation
	5	Saint Margaret		9	Saint Catherine of Alexandria
Outer Circle	10	Foliage		18	Foliage
	11	Saint Andrew		19	Saint Matthew
	12	Saint Peter		20	Saint Bartholomew
	13	Saint Paul		21	Saint James the Less
	14	Foliage		22	Foliage
	15	Saint Thomas		23	Saint Matthias
	16	Saint John		24	Saint Simon
	17	Saint James the Great		25	Saint Philip
East	26	Queen Anne of Bohemia (?)	South	34	King Richard II (?)
	27	Angel of Saint Mark		35	Angel of Saint Luke
	28	Red Lion		36	Queen Eleanor of Castille (?)
	29	A Hairy Hybrid		37	King Edward I (?)
North	30	King Henry VI (?)	West	38	Queen Margaret of Anjou (?)
	31	Angel of Saint John		39	Angel of Saint Matthew
	32	A Saracen		40	A Physician
	33	A Gentleman		41	A Physician

The Great Hospital, Norwich
A description of the roof bosses in the vaulting of the south transept of St Helen's church

St Giles's Hospital, now known as The Great Hospital, was founded in October 1249 by Walter Suffield, bishop of Norwich, 1244-57. The hospital was built to the north-east of the cathedral on a site north of Holme Street, now Bishopgate. Succeeding bishops, especially Henry Despenser, 1369-1406, Walter Lyhart, 1446-1472, and James Goldwell, 1472-99, were influential in adding to and indeed altering the original set of buildings established by the founder. At the end of the fourteenth century Despenser rebuilt the chancel of St Helen's church, and a hundred years later Goldwell, among other renovations, created a vaulted south transept over a chantry chapel containing a rich and spectacular array of roof bosses.

Walter Suffield dedicated his hospital to St Giles, the patron saint of beggars and cripples, and one to whom many miracles of healing were attributed. Included also in the dedication were the Virgin Mary and her mother, St Anne. The cult of the Virgin Mary and her mother grew in popularity throughout Europe in the thirteenth century. In the Norwich diocese chapels and churches were increasingly dedicated to the Virgin Mary and to St Anne. Bishop Suffield himself had been responsible for ordering the demolition of the easternmost apsidal chapel in the cathedral and its replacement with a very large Early English Lady Chapel, *c.*1250. And before the middle of the fourteenth century two additional chapels had been added to the presbytery area, St Anne's Chapel to the north, *c.*1330, now demolished, and the Bauchun Chapel to the south, *c.*1327-29, dedicated to Our Lady of Pity. The fifteenth-

---

*The coded references in parentheses are to the numbering as set out in the CD-ROM Norwich Cathedral Roof Bosses, Images by Julia Hedgecoe, Text by Martial Rose, Norwich, 2000. (See over.)

century stone vaulting in the Bauchun Chapel extends over two bays; the central boss of the southern bay is of the Assumption of the Virgin (BC12)*, and the central boss of the northern bay is of the Coronation of the Virgin (BC36). The story told by the other forty or so roof bosses in this chapel is of a calumniated empress who, in pleading her cause with the Virgin Mary, is given the power of healing, and in particular the healing of lepers. A corbel in the Bauchun Chapel is thought to represent William Seckyngton, Master of the Great Hospital in 1430, who also acted as the bishop's corrector general, using the Bauchun Chapel as the consistory court. The elaborate refurbishment of the chantry chapel in St Helen's south transept was most likely undertaken shortly after the completion of the re-roofing of the Bauchun Chapel. The work was almost certainly put in hand under the direction and with the financial support of Bishop Goldwell. It would have been at the same time, about 1480, that the bishop was planning his own chantry chapel in the cathedral and also inaugurating a major change to the presbytery roof, which was to house 128 roof bosses, most of which represented gold wells, rebuses on the bishop's name. Among the few bosses not bearing the bishop's rebus is one splendid carving of the

Bishop Goldwell's coat of arms, a presbytery roof boss in Norwich Cathedral

Virgin in Glory (P28). Goldwell's coat of arms, displayed on one of the cathedral's presbytery roof bosses (P4) is also prominent on one of the clustered columns in the nave of St Helen's. James Goldwell's standing was international. He had acted as Edward IV's secretary of state and negotiated peace with France in 1471. In the following year he was appointed ambassador in Rome and also served as principal recorder to the papal court, from which post, while in Rome, he was elevated to the see of Norwich in 1472. His brother, Nicholas, served as Master of St Giles's for a brief period in 1497/8, and as executor of his brother's will was charged with the duty of arranging the endowment of his brother's chantry and annual obit at the Hospital. James Goldwell proved to be one of the most generous benefactors of St Giles's. The corona of roof bosses in the south transept chapel is perhaps today his most signal legacy to the Hospital.

The stone vaulted ceiling of the chantry chapel comprises a series of stone ribs locked together by a number of keystones, or roof bosses, which are lowered into position from above. The carving on the bosses was probably undertaken at this stage. The spaces between the ribs were then filled in. The pattern of the vaulting in the chapel is unlike any of the ribbed vaulting of the late fifteenth century in the cathedral, although it is likely that the work was carried out by some of the same craftsmen. Each of the fourteen bays

St Helen's Chapel, north-east vaulting

in the nave of the cathedral contains twenty-four bosses arranged in an elliptical stellar pattern around a central, larger boss. The central boss announces the theme of the story to be told by eighteen bosses in the bay. The other six are of foliate or floriate design. In this chantry chapel the pattern is that of a crown holding within it a circular stellar arrangement of the bosses. The central, larger boss is of the Coronation of the Virgin, and the subject matter of the surrounding bosses is subservient to, but reinforces, this theme. An outstanding feature of the thousand or so roof bosses in Norwich Cathedral is the extensive nature of their story-telling. Here the story-telling concentrates on the Virgin Mary. There was already a Lady Chapel on the north side of St Helen's, and with so many of the chapels in the cathedral also devoted to the Virgin Mary, it is not surprising that this entirely refurbished chapel in St Helen's should underline that devotion. But it does so in an unusual way.

There are many sources of the apocryphal life of the Virgin Mary; perhaps one of the most widely known in the Middle Ages and that used by scholars, preachers, poets, playwrights and artists is *The Golden Legend,* written in the mid-thirteenth century by Jacob of Voragine, archbishop of Genoa. It tells the stories of the saints and especially expands on the life

Norwich Cathedral cloister - foliate boss

of the Virgin Mary, giving an account of her early life as well as dwelling in some detail on her death and assumption. The last events in the life of the Virgin were celebrated in the liturgy of the Church and also in multiple art-forms, including drama. The fifteenth-century *N-Town Play*, a Norfolk mystery cycle with passages which deal extensively with the life of the Virgin Mary, contains a long, and elaborately staged, play, *The Assumption of the Virgin*. The Death (CNE3), and Coronation of the Virgin (CNE5) are subjects treated by the cloister bosses in the north walk of Norwich Cathedral, and as previously mentioned carvings related to the Assumption and Coronation appear in the Bauchun Chapel.

The treatment of the Coronation of the Virgin in the carvings in St Helen's presents two concentric circles of bosses having particular relevance to the central carving, which is double the size of the encircling bosses. Beyond these two circles, at each of the four cardinal points, are groupings of four bosses of local and national significance. The inner circle comprises eight bosses: four relating to Christ's life and four depicting saints. The four relating to Christ's life show the Annunciation, the Nativity, the Resurrection and the Ascension, which together with the Coronation were referred to as The Five Joys of Mary. Alternating with these scenes from Christ's life are four saints: St Margaret, St Catherine, St Edmund, and St Edward. The outer ring comprises sixteen bosses four of which, east, south, west and north, are foliate. Each of the remaining twelve depicts one of the apostles. The arch of Norwich Cathedral's Erpingham Gate, built in the second quarter of the fifteenth century, has two orders of mouldings: the inner contains images of the twelve apostles, each housed within a canopied niche; and the outer comprises twelve images of female saints, among which are St Catherine and St Margaret.

Perhaps there is more significance to be attached to the numbers of the roof bosses in the vaulting than might be ascribed to their architectural need or pattern formation. There are eight bosses in the inner ring, sixteen in the outer ring, and sixteen on the periphery, at the four cardinal points. Arrangements are in pairs, fours, eights, twelves and sixteens. There are twenty-four bosses in the two circles surrounding The Coronation of the Virgin. The twelve apostles are seated on thrones as are the saints. They are in solemn conclave, and the setting has associations with a passage in Revelation (4. vv 2-11) in which St John has a vision of Christ enthroned in heaven with four and twenty crowned elders seated below. In St Helen's there are forty bosses in all surrounding the central carving. The number forty, too, has biblical resonances.

St Catherine of Alexandria and St Margaret of Antioch are frequently paired in medieval art forms associated with the Virgin

Mary, examples of which are to be seen in the painting on the Ante-Reliquary Chapel arch in the cathedral, *c.*1300, and in the Thornham Parva retable, *c.*1335, a retable linked with the frontal, its sister painting in Paris, which is devoted to scenes from the life of the Virgin (Frontal, Musée de Cluny). St Catherine and St Margaret are also paired on a fifteenth-century bench-end in St Mary's, Ufford, Suffolk. Also within that inner circle in the St Helen's vaulting are St Edward and St Edmund, saints who with the Virgin Mary are closely linked with King Richard II, as is evident in the Wilton Diptych, *c.*1396. And, again, these saints are carved in the Norwich cathedral cloister bosses (St Edmund, CEB3, CNH7: St Edward, CNI3). St Edmund, king of East Anglia, appears also in the tabernacle carving above the Prior's Door in the north-east corner of the cathedral cloisters. King Richard II and his young queen, Anne of Bohemia, the daughter of the Emperor Charles IV, visited Norwich in the summer of 1383, and it is possible that the carving in the vaulting of

The eagle ceiling, St Helen's Church

this chantry chapel reflects that visit as does the painting of the eagles, a symbol of the Empire, in the 252 panels on the ceiling of the chancel.

In the Middle Ages the premier Marian shrine in England was that of Our Lady of Walsingham, which was visited by Henry III (1207-1272) on many occasions, and subsequently by most of the pre-Reformation kings and queens of England. The pilgrims to Walsingham often passed through Norwich on their way. It is therefore understandable that these two centres of religious iconography might have influenced each other. When in 1512 Erasmus visited the Walsingham shrine he noted that 'on a gold altarpiece stood a representation of the Virgin in the centre, flanked by images of two angels, St Edward, St Katherine, St Edmund and St Margaret' (Marks 2004, 196).

While the four saints mentioned above play an integral role within the inner ring of the St Helen's chantry chapel vaulting, the outer ring comprises images of the twelve apostles who according to tradition were called to the bedside of the Virgin Mary to witness her death and assumption. This story is dramatized in *The N-Town Play* in *The Assumption of Mary*. Among the apostles depicted in the bosses are St Paul and St Matthias, but not included is St Jude. Both inner and outer circles of the crown affirm the Coronation of the Virgin. And that special English affirmation is underlined by the canonised kings, St Edmund and St Edward, and by the other royal figures which are carved on the peripheral roof bosses. The ascription to Edward I, Eleanor of Castile, Richard II, Anne of Bohemia, Henry VI, and Margaret of Anjou have come about by a mixture of conjecture and tradition. There is little historical basis for such identification.

It is probable that this corona of roof bosses, executed with consummate craftsmanship with no expense spared, might have provided the decorative vaulting to a chantry chapel for Bishop Goldwell himself. He had already made provision for a sumptuous chantry chapel in the presbytery of the cathedral, but there were reasons why he thought his wishes, that chantry priests and bedesmen might pray daily for his soul after his death, might be more conscientiously carried out in St Helen's. Goldwell's vaulting of the cathedral presbytery had broken with the tradition of studding the rib-work with a series of narrative roof bosses. Narrative plays no dominant role in this St Helen's chantry chapel vaulting. Instead the corona, centred on the Coronation of the Virgin, offers an image for devotion and supplication. This grouping of bosses would have presented the parishioners and the frail inmates of St Giles's Hospital with a focus for their prayers, seeking intercession from the Virgin to their Father in heaven, that their petitions should be answered and their ailments assuaged.

In 1944 John Chaplin undertook the cleaning and the repainting of the chantry chapel roof bosses (Rawcliffe 1999, 290) and he explained how he set about this task perched on the top of a moveable scaffold, clearing away centuries of grime with soap and water (Chaplin 1949). He discovered that all the original colours, found to be painted with an oil medium, probably linseed, could be traced, and he remarked especially on the gold leaf, brush gold, and the Tudor reds and greens. He noticed that parts of the vaulting were encrusted with what he took to be soot, and wondered whether this deposit might have been part of the legacy of Robert Kett's uprising in 1549. On August 1 of this year Kett and his men left their camp on Mousehold Heath and attacked the city from the east. The fragile fortifications of the Bishop's gate and those at The Great Hospital were soon breached, the houses in Holme Street set alight, and the south side of St Helen's church severely damaged by fire. The south aisle of the church was never rebuilt. But the chantry chapel, although damaged, survived. It may well have been that those deposits of soot, in consequence of the fire in 1549, contributed substantially to the preservation of the vaulting.

When Munro Cautley was preparing his book on *Norfolk Churches*, published in 1949, he visited St Helen's to discover that scaffolding had been erected in the chantry chapel. He was able to inspect the roof bosses at close quarters and commented 'the original colour is on them and they are now being freshened up'. And Nikolaus Pevsner in 1962 confirmed that the original colours had been preserved. This five-hundred year legacy is precious indeed. The colours are from a restricted palette: browns, reds, greys, greens, golds, white and black. There are few blues. But it was not just the preservation of the colours that Cautley, Pevsner, and many others have rejoiced at, but the exquisite craftsmanship of the whole design and the skill and accomplishment evident in the sculpted bosses.

A further unusual aspect of the vaulting in this chantry chapel is that this set of roof bosses, although slightly damaged in the course of more than five hundred years, has not suffered noticeably from the vandalism of the sixteenth and seventeenth centuries, in spite of the fact that the focus of so much of that iconoclasm was against images of the Virgin Mary. A few hands may be missing, apostles' attributes broken, but the original sculpting of the figures is intact. The high-vaulted roof bosses of Norwich Cathedral escaped the vandals' attention because of their being over seventy feet above ground level. The cloister roof bosses, on the other hand, only fifteen feet above ground level, were severely damaged, and that damage was concentrated mainly on knocking off the heads of the carved figures. The roof bosses in St Helen's chantry chapel are about twenty feet from the ground, and well within the range of a desecrator's seventeen-foot pike. Why then were they left unscathed?

In May 1538 the Norwich Benedictine priory, as a result of Henry VIII's statutes of Reformation, became a secular community under the control of a dean and chapter. The images within the cathedral and cloisters which were thought to promote superstition and idolatry were spasmodically, over the next hundred or so years, subjected to 'principled' desecration. St Giles's Hospital, however, was treated very differently. In 1535 by Act of Parliament the control of the Hospital passed to the King and, apart from the change of Master in 1537, little was altered until the accession of Edward VI in 1547. In March of this year the young King ceded control of the Hospital to the Mayor, Sheriffs and citizens of Norwich. The Hospital became a refuge for forty poor and sick residents of the city. And it is probably because of these civic, rather than ecclesiastical, concerns and responsibilities that the premises were not subjected to the zealous hands of the iconoclasts.

In the following description of the individual bosses many analogies are drawn with other medieval art especially with work extant in Norwich Cathedral. Just as the bishops of Norwich took so lively an interest in St Giles's Hospital, so the work that they commissioned there was undertaken by the same craftsmen who laboured on similar projects in the larger institution. So many of the subjects being treated were identical in both places. But whereas one can detect apprentice work in some of the cathedral carving, say, in the Bauchun Chapel, work nearly contemporaneous with that of the chantry chapel carving, no inferior hand is discernible in the St Helen's vaulting. In conception and execution it is of the highest order. It is a rare treasure, and one to be cherished.

Photographer, Bruce Benedict, at work

Boss Number 1 — The Coronation of the Virgin

The Coronation of the Virgin was one of the most popular themes in medieval iconography, in church paintings, illuminated manuscripts, monumental brasses, and carvings in wood, ivory, alabaster and stone. The Virgin after her death and assumption into heaven received her heavenly crown seated sometimes between the Father and the Son, with the Holy Ghost in the form of a dove hovering above, and sometimes, as here, receiving a blessing from the Son. It was such an image that brought great comfort to medieval Christendom. And indeed it still brings comfort to millions of Christians today. The Virgin is reverenced for her powers of intercession on behalf of the women in childbirth, and for those nearing death and about to face their final judgement. When St Michael weighs in his scales the souls of the dead, through the intercession of the Virgin Mary, Our Lady of Mercy, her rosary might also be placed in the scales to ease the path of those souls heavenward (Cheetham 134). The sick, too, prayed to the Virgin for the recovery of their health. Among the parishioners and the ailing inmates of St Helen's were a great many who might look to this roof boss image of the Virgin with feelings of love, relief, and support.

As the centre boss of the pattern forming the crown in the vaulting of the chantry chapel, it is at least twice as large as any of the attendant carvings. It forms part of the keystone for the junction of eight stone ribs. Thirteen angels surround the two central figures of Christ and the Virgin Mary. Most of the angels show some part of their elegantly shaped golden-feathered wings, and above each angel is a fan-shaped, stylised cloud, layered in places, to produce a coffered effect. The angels beneath and either side of the coronation play a variety of musical instruments, some plucking strings, one using a bow, and another turning the handle of a miniature hurdy-gurdy. The angels above are linked by scrolls which twist and turn from one to another. Two of the angels are singing from office books which

they hold in front of them. Of the angel directly beneath the feet of the Virgin and Christ only the head appears, but it is encircled by a fluted blue cloud which gives the effect of a ruff. No wording on the scrolls is decipherable, but originally it would probably have extolled the Virgin's virtues. There is no representation in this carving of the Father or the Holy Ghost. The Virgin sits on Christ's right* hand side. Her crown is set over her head-dress which is similar to that which she wears in the carving of The Nativity (Boss Number 2). She wears a capacious cloak which is parted at the neck to expose her gown beneath, but covers her lap and knees, and lies in gathered folds beneath her feet. The round neckline of her gown is decorated with a braided band which extends down the front of her dress. The Virgin's arms are crossed in front of her breast as an act of submission, and her head, turned towards Christ, is inclined modestly. Christ who is also crowned holds up the first two fingers of his right hand in blessing. He is looking outwards. He is moustached and bearded. He wears a cloak over a much-pleated gown. His left hand rests on an orb, a symbol of the universe. His feet are bare; neither hands nor feet bear any signs of the stigmata.

The representation of this scene with its many varied forms appeared in a multitude of churches in the Middle Ages. Ann Nichols has recorded such representations in Norfolk churches in her *Early Art of Norfolk*, Michigan, 2002. The two representations of this theme in Norwich Cathedral are in the cloister (CNE5) and in the Bauchun Chapel (BC36). These both include the presence of the Trinity. The St Helen's boss achieves a more balanced serenity with just the two main characters, the Virgin and Christ, placed centrally with two angels either side. Above are six angels, arranged in two patterned threesomes. And beneath the main figures are another three angels, the two on the outside playing their instruments, and all three providing a footstool for Christ and the Virgin.

---

* 'Right' and 'left' refer to the viewer's right and left except, as in cases such as this, where the direction is from the carved figure's standpoint.

Boss Number 2 — The Nativity

The birth of Christ is the second of Mary's 'Joys'. Here the scene is set against a panel of planked fencing. The top of each plank is pointed, and the whole painted red. This manner of fencing, seen frequently in medieval art forms such as in the carving in the nave vaulting of Norwich Cathedral of Christ's Agony in the Garden (NK1), is usually indicative of an outdoor setting. Four figures are carved against this background. Mary appears on the left and Joseph on the right. Between them stands a woman, holding in her hands what probably represents a large bath-towel. The Christ-child sits in front of her on a much larger cloth or towel. The towel is coloured cream, the larger cloth a light blue. The infant Christ holds up his thumb and forefinger of his right hand in blessing. To the left behind the Virgin, resting on the arm of her seat, is a small barrel-like object with a red cover.

Behind Joseph is a section of wattle fencing. He is seated, his left hand resting upon his stick. He is bearded and wears a skull cap. He looks outward as does the woman standing next to him, a white veil and wimple cover her head and shoulders. The Virgin, also seated, holds the infant's right arm and on him directs her gaze. The

Virgin's hair falls from beneath her head-dress which is crimped in front. Three articles are set out at the base of the carving, the middle one of which appears to be a tankard full to the brim.

The scene in all probability depicts the moment when the midwife, having bathed the infant, hands him back to his mother. In apocryphal stories associated with the birth of Christ, midwives are frequently introduced, even given names such as Salome and Zebel (Cheetham 179). The midwives in *The N-Town Play*, a mystery cycle of Norfolk provenance, are called Salome and Zelomy. One such midwife is seen in an illumination from *The Holkham Bible Picture*, c.1330, Folio 12v. In the great east window of St Peter Mancroft, Norwich, is a stained glass depiction of The Nativity, c.1485, in which, as Mary nurses her child and Joseph sits with folded arms, a midwife kneels to warm a towel over a brazier. The two midwives featured in the East Harling stained glass Nativity, 1463-1480, wear head-dresses very similar to that worn by this St Helen's midwife.

The Nativity in the east window at St Peter Mancroft with detail of the midwife warming swaddling clothes by a brazier.

St Anastasia, who used to be commemorated in the Second Mass for Christmas Day, is sometimes referred to as the holy midwife (Binski 2005, 196).

This carving is unique in its setting, having two additional carvings set between the upper part of the rib vaulting: the first portrays three angels holding in front of them a scroll and looking down on the Nativity; and the other shows the manger with the ox and the ass. The manger, set above the ox and the ass, has red bars in which is seen fodder for the animals.

Boss Number 3 — Saint Edmund

King Edmund (*c.*840-69) became King of East Anglia by 865. He resisted the Danish invasion of 869, but was defeated in battle and captured. He was offered his life if he would agree to share his kingdom with the Danes and abandon his Christian faith. On his refusal he was shot to death by arrows and then decapitated. Legend has it that a wolf guarded his head from the Danes, and would only yield it to the Saxons. The martyr's body was taken to the abbey, now known as Bury St Edmunds, where the saint's relics rapidly became the goal of many pilgrims.

Here St Edmund is crowned. His hair and beard are brown tinted with gold. Over his shoulders he wears a grey-green tippet under which is a full, red gown, its ample skirting streaked with gold. St Edmund is seated on a throne and in his left hand he holds the haft of an arrow, the top part of which has broken off. The large barbed arrow-head rests against his left knee. In his right hand is the fragment of the broken scroll, bearing his name, which would have curled about the carving, joining up with the rest of the lettering behind the Saint's head.

In the crown-like design of the chantry chapel vaulting St Edmund is placed diametrically opposite St Edward the Confessor. The two saints are paired here as they are on the Wilton Diptych. They were the patron saints of England until replaced by St George in the fourteenth century. But they continued to be greatly venerated, especially as English saints. Richard II's devotion to them was especially marked, and no region showed more devotion to St Edmund than East Anglia where his martyrdom occurred and where his relics remained. Images of St Edmund abound in this region. They can, for instance, be seen in stained glass in Holy Trinity, Long Melford, in panel painting in St Mary's church, Kersey, Suffolk, and in two of the cloister carvings in Norwich Cathedral, CEB3, and CNI7.

In the Thornham Parva retable St Edmund is paired with John the Baptist and in the tabernacle carving over the Prior's Door of

Norwich Cathedral he again appears near John the Baptist. But here in St Helen's he is paired with St Edward because both are crowned kings, both are English, and both contribute to the central coronation theme in a markedly English and Christian way.

Boss Number 4 — The Resurrection

The Resurrection carving represents the third Joy of Mary. Christ steps from the tomb. He is dressed in a brown robe which falls from his shoulders to reveal the upper part of his body. The wound made by the spear thrust is evident, but no stigmata on his hands or his foot are apparent. Christ has a crown of thorns on his head. He is moustached and bearded and his right hand is held up in blessing; in his left hand he grasps the haft of a stout cross-staff, the bottom part of which has broken away. From the cross at the top flies a pennon with the red cross of St George. The four soldiers have taken up positions at the four corners of the tomb. Two of them seem to be sleeping, top left and bottom right, and the other two stare straight ahead. Three of the soldiers are helmeted, but the one at the bottom left, wearing a pleated tunic, has a more sophisticated appearance. It is upon his body that Christ treads with his right foot as he emerges from the tomb. The stationing of the four soldiers at each of the corners of the tomb might reflect the way this scene was performed in *The N-Town Play*, 34, 216-229*, and the manner in which Christ strides from the tomb steadying himself with the cross-staff and using the body of one of the soldiers as a stepping-stone might also reflect dramatic performance. In the plays about the resurrection the soldiers say that although they could see Christ rise from the tomb they were powerless to do anything about it (*The N-Town Play*, 35,193-216). Here two soldiers seem to be asleep; the one on the right at the base of the boss sleeps with his head upon his hands which rest on the hilt of his sword.

The two bosses in Norwich Cathedral, CEB5 and NM4, share in general terms the same explosive energy engendered by the bursting from the tomb. This representation, showing the soldiers at the four corners of the tomb, and Christ with the cross-staff in one hand and stepping on one of the soldiers lying in front of the tomb, is repeated in many of the alabasters on this theme (Cheetham 199-206).

The tomb is a rectangular sarcophagus, but the sculptor has given it a curved front to harmonise with the curvature of the boss. The fretwork of patterned holes in the front of the tomb indicates that it is a feretory, such as might hold the relics of a saint, and at which pilgrims might kneel and feel the spirit of the saint visit them through the apertures.

Within the groin of the ribs, above the main part of the carving, is an angel dressed in feathered tunic and wings. The angel stands above the empty tomb and holds up with his right hand the tomb's ridged and polished lid.

*The N-Town Play, Play 34 Guarding the Sepulchre, 216-229. The soldiers declare which corner of the tomb they will guard.

Boss Number 5 — St Margaret of Antioch

St Margaret is reputed to have been martyred in the early fourth century under the reign of the Roman Emperor Diocletian. No verifiable fact is known about her, but the legend is that she was imprisoned for her defiance in clinging to her Christian faith. Then Satan in the form of a dragon swallowed her. But when she made the sign of the cross the dragon's belly burst open and she was delivered unharmed. Her attributes are a book and a cross-staff. Most images of St Margaret show her thrusting her cross-staff into the mouth of a dragon. St Margaret was often invoked by women in childbirth.

In this carving St Margaret is crowned and is dressed in a gown over which is a cloak covering her left shoulder and upper part of her body. She is seated and in her right hand holds the haft of a broken cross-staff which is thrust into the mouth of a dragon, whose rows of long sharp teeth bite into the staff. In St Margaret's left hand she holds another object which is now unidentifiable. Behind her head a scroll is unfurled with lettering stating the subject of the carving.

Images of St Margaret abounded in the Middle Ages, and they are to be found in many churches in East Anglia. They appear as wall-paintings, wood carvings, painted screens, retables and in stained-glass windows, such as that in St Mary's, North Tuddenham. As mentioned in the introduction, an image of St Margaret with her attributes is to be seen in one of the niches in the Erpingham Gate. There is also in St Helen's church a bold carving of St Margaret and the dragon, serving as a bench-end, installed during the time that John Hecker was Master, in the 1520s.

The pairing with St Catherine, as has already been noted, was common in the Middle Ages. In the pattern of St Helen's vaulting both St Margaret and St Catherine are seated on thrones, both are crowned, and they are placed, as St Edmund and St Edward, diametrically opposite each other, either side of the Coronation of the Virgin. Whereas St Edmund and St Edward have a special English provenance, St Margaret and St Catherine in Christian iconography resonate universally.

Front and back view of St Margaret's bench-end in St Helen's Church

Photograph: Elizabeth Armstrong

Boss Number 6 — The Ascension of Christ

The Ascension of Christ is the fourth of the Virgin Mary's Five Joys. Ascension Day is one of the most important feasts in the Christian Year, and is kept on the sixth Thursday after Easter. According to the account in Acts 1.3 the Ascension took place forty days after the Resurrection, and tradition has it that the event was enacted on the Mount of Olives. This late fifteenth century carving shares most of the features common to other art forms interpreting the event. Twelve apostles are gathered around the Virgin, who stands in the midst of them. Over her red gown she wears a draped overmantle. Both hands would have been raised, but her left hand has broken off at the wrist. She looks upward. Six apostles stand each side of her, some looking upwards, some at the Virgin and some elsewhere. The two apostles recognisable in this assembly are St Peter and St John. St Peter stands to the left of the Virgin. He can be distinguished by his bald-headedness or by a tonsure. It was tradition that St Peter received the tonsure the moment that Christ washed his feet at the Last Supper (*Holkham Bible Picture Book*, Folio 28). St John is distinguished as the only apostle who is beardless. All the apostles, whose hands are seen, have them raised in prayer.

In many representations of this event the top of the mountain from which Christ ascends is visible, as in the two Norwich Cathedral roof bosses, CNC5 and NM10. Also in some art forms the stigmata on Christ's feet can be seen as well as his footprints on top of the mountain (CNC5). Here, however, neither mountain-top nor stigmata are evident, but instead, surrounding the feet and the lower half of Christ's gown, is an impressive array of stylised clouds of fan-vaulting design. Similarly designed clouds appear in the St Helen's Coronation, and they provide, as here, a halo effect. As they are layered, one below another either side of Christ's disappearing feet, they give the appearance of a coffered ceiling, a set of pendants, framing the scene within. The design effect is similar, in a more modest way, to the early sixteenth century fan vaulting in King's College Chapel, Cambridge, and, more particularly, with the pendant fan vaulting in the Lady Chapel of King Henry VII in Westminster Abbey.

Boss Number 7 — Edward the Confessor

This carving of St Edward the Confessor is placed diametrically opposite that of St Edmund. Edward and Edmund are the two canonized kings of England. King Edward reigned from 1042 to 1066. Here Edward is enthroned. He is seen as a relatively young man, crowned, with auburn hair and beard. Beneath a grey tippet he is wearing a dark brown gown drawn in at the waist by a jewelled girdle. His hands emerge from voluminous sleeves. In his left hand he holds a substantial and weapon-like sceptre, the knobbed base of which rests on his left knee while the sceptre's head touches his hair and crown. In his right hand he holds the end of a scroll which is unfurled behind his head and extends to the further armrest of the throne. The lettering on the scroll reads 'S Edward'. Also in his right hand is held a ring, the top half of which is missing. The sceptre and the ring are the main attributes of St Edward the Confessor. It is said that the king gave his ring to a hair-shirted, barefoot pilgrim, a reincarnation of St John the Evangelist. Edward, prominent in the Wilton Diptych, is seen there holding a ring in his left hand.

In the north walk of Norwich Cathedral cloisters there are two roof bosses illustrating other aspects of Edward's life: his auspicious birth (CNG7), and his Christian devotion, as the King, kneeling at a prayer-desk, attends Mass (CNI3).

Edward the Confessor was favoured by King Henry III as the patron saint of England, a role he shared with King Edmund, until subsequently superseded by St George in the fourteenth century.

Boss Number 8 — The Annunciation

Of the Five Joys of the Virgin the Annunciation is the first. The composition resembles that of some late fifteenth-century alabasters (Cheetham 170,171), with the angel kneeling to the left of the Virgin, who, half turning at the salutation, holds up her right hand in a gesture of surprise or sense of unworthiness. Between the angel and the Virgin is an elongated flower vase with a bulbous middle section. From the vase grows the stout stalk of a lily having small offshoots on either side, culminating in five large flowers that blossom at the very top of the carving, above the heads of the two participants. These five flowers may represent the Five Joys of the Virgin. The lily, a symbol of purity for both the Virgin and her Son, features also at times as the cross itself on which Christ is crucified, as in the late fifteenth-century Long Melford stained-glass window. In medieval times there was a belief that the Annunciation and the Crucifixion took place on the same day, 25th March. In many images of the Annunciation the Holy Ghost is seen as a dove winging its way towards the Virgin Mary. Here the dove appears on the right almost at the ear of the Virgin. In the stained-glass Annunciation in the east window of St Peter Mancroft, Norwich, behind the dove is the image of the unborn Christ-child carrying over his shoulder a tau cross.

The Annunciation scene from the east window in St Peter Mancroft Church with detail (left) of the dove followed by the unborn Christ-child carrying a tau cross

According to St Luke, 1.v 28, the angel greets Mary with the words 'Hail, thou that art highly favoured, the Lord is with thee: blessed art thou among women.' In many scenes of the Annunciation these words in Latin are written on a scroll. Here there is no wording to be seen, but a characteristic which relates this carving to the alabasters previously mentioned is the way the scroll entwines round the lily. The angel holds the bottom of the scroll with his left hand. His right hand is held up in salutation. The Virgin who is standing by a lectern, which is on the extreme right of the carving and on which rests an open book, is dressed in a grey, round-necked gown over which a brown cloak falls from her shoulders across the front of her body. The angel's great wings seem to enfold from behind both the angel and the Virgin.

The Tree of Jesse demonstrated in art forms how from the line of David sprang the Virgin and Christ, her son. The lineage of Christ is shown as a tree growing from Jesse, as he lies asleep. Its branches reach to David, his son, and so through the successive generations that culminate in the Annunciation and at the very top the Coronation of the Virgin by Christ. Such an illustration can be seen in the Ormesby Psalter, Folio 9v, *c.*1320. In the two alabaster representations of the Annunciation referred to above the Virgin is crowned as she receives the angel's salutation. In this St Helen's representation she is not. But in all three instances the stout lily stalk is characterised by a number of offshoots as though the lily itself represents the Tree of Jesse and its upper flowering will lead through the crucifixion and resurrection of Christ to the ultimate crowning by Christ of the Virgin in heaven.

Boss Number 9 — St Catherine of Alexandria

St Catherine, according to tradition, was martyred in Alexandria in the early fourth century. She was put to death by the Roman Emperor Maxentius because of her persistent protests against the persecution of Christians. She was tied to a wheel, tortured and finally beheaded. Great devotion centred on her during the Middle Ages, above all in France, during the time of the Crusades. In the fifteenth century Joan of Arc's belief, that she heard constantly the voices of St Catherine and St Margaret urging her on to drive the English forces out of France, might well have been part of that crusading tradition. St Catherine's attribute is a spiked wheel.

Young women, wheelwrights, attorneys, and scholars regarded St Catherine as their patron saint.

St Catherine is crowned. She is seated upon a throne the back of which is decorated with large red roses. Behind her head an open scroll declares her name. The top half of her body is clad in a close-fitting grey garment over which is a reddish-brown pleated garment, in the style of a cotehardie. Her arms are broken off above the wrists, but it might be assumed that her right hand held the spiked wheel and her left a sword, the symbol of her having been beheaded. It is perhaps part of the sword that remains visible on the scroll to the right of St Catherine's head.

The iconographic pairing of St Catherine and St Margaret in association with the Virgin Mary is not infrequent. As has already been mentioned it appears in the early fourteenth-century wall painting in the Ante-Reliquary Chapel of Norwich Cathedral, and also in an altarpiece of the Joys of the Virgin at Avilés, Spain (Cheetham 84). Devotion to St Catherine was strong in Norwich. An early thirteenth century cathedral chapel in the south transept was dedicated to her, and a city church, St Catherine Newgate. In the cathedral cloisters two roof bosses portray her martyrdom, CNJ6, CNK1.

Among the medieval alabasters that have survived there are few of St Margaret, but very many of St Catherine, many of which depict her in prison, or being tortured, or being beheaded. Here both saints are in repose. Within the inner ring of bosses in the chantry chapel they sit on thrones, wearing their crowns, and they are balanced by the two saintly kings who likewise sit on thrones. Four other bosses in this group are of the four Joys of Mary with the fifth, the Coronation of the Virgin, at the very centre. It is as though the sainted kings and queens have been invited to witness the fifth and final Joy of the Virgin Mary.

Bosses Numbered 10, 14, 18, and 22 —
The Foliate Bosses

The four roof bosses on which foliage is carved, without any human or animal representation, are in the outer circle of sixteen bosses. In this group there are twelve, four groups of three, showing each of the twelve apostles, and four foliate carvings, each appearing at a cardinal point. And it is these foliate bosses that link the central coronal pattern to each of the terminal group of four bosses, east, south, west, and north.

In the vault carvings in Norwich Cathedral foliate and floriate designs are frequently employed to punctuate a sequence of historiated, or story-telling, carvings. A similar principle might operate here.

The whorl-like design of oak leaves in 10, and acanthus in 22, have distinct analogues in the much earlier cloister carvings (CEC1, CEF5, and CEG2).

No 10	*No 14*
No 18	*No 22*

Boss Number 11 — St Andrew

St Andrew is placed next to his brother St Peter, Boss Number 12. The carving is relatively undamaged: St Andrew's left hand is missing. The whole representation is striking in its effect, with the careful depiction of the saint's hair and wavy, forked beard, pleated red robe with capacious sleeves lined in a cream-coloured material, and the rich golden cloak.

St Andrew is seated on a grey bench or throne. In his right hand he holds one end of a brown saltire cross. The saltire cross is his attribute. His head and shoulders are framed by a scroll on which his name is written in letters of black and red. Beneath the scroll to the right of St Andrew's shoulder are red fruit, perhaps apples, and above the scroll swathes of red apples are carved into the groins between the ribs.

Boss Number 12 — St Peter

St Peter is identified by the name on the broken scroll above his head, and also by his holding in his left hand two very large keys. In the Scriptures St Peter often acts as the mouthpiece of Christ's disciples, and his name appears at the head of the list of the Apostles. It was to Peter that Christ said 'on this rock will I build my church ...and I will give thee the keys of the kingdom of heaven' (Matthew, 16, vv 18,19). The keys are St Peter's attribute.

The scroll, which is missing on the left side, carries the name 'Petrus'. The carving is unusual in showing St Peter beardless and with a page-like hair style. Over a round-necked garment is wrapped a mantle with many horizontal folds. St Peter is seated on a red bench or throne with armrests. His right hand and part of one of the keys have broken off. Behind the saint are the same red fruits seen in the carving of St Andrew.

Boss Number 13 — St Paul

The Apostle Paul is framed by a semicircle of an unbroken scroll that declares his name in letters of red and black.

His hair and beard are auburn. Over a grey-green robe he wears a red cloak which falls over his left shoulder and is wrapped round his body just above the waist. Paul holds the hilt of a broad-bladed sword in his left hand. The top half of the blade has broken off, but the part near the point appears against the scroll. The sword is St Paul's attribute. It is said that, because he was a Roman citizen when he was condemned to death in Rome, rather than suffer crucifixion, he was decapitated by a sword.

A dark rugged background containing the semblance of fruit is worked from behind the Apostle into the groins between the boss's receiving ribs.

Boss Number 15 — St Thomas

St Thomas, like the other apostles, is seen seated on a bench or throne. An unfurled scroll reaches from left to right, framing the upper part of the carving, bearing the saint's name in letters of brown and red. Thomas is bearded. He wears a grey gown beneath a brown cloak, which falls from his right shoulder, covering the lower part of his body as well as being looped over his right hand. In his left hand he holds the bottom part of the haft of a spear, the upper part of which has broken off. The most common attributes of the saint are a square, to denote his apocryphal building activities, and also a spear (Cheetham 152), a sword and a cross.

Boss Number 16 — St John

In this carving St John the Evangelist has short, curly auburn hair and is beardless. He is dressed in a red gown, gathered at the waist. A brown cloak with a green lining falls over both shoulders.

St John's left forearm and hand are missing. In his right hand is the base of a chalice. The Evangelist is seated on a red bench with armrests either side. The scroll which would have been unfurled around the upper part of the boss now shows two fragments only: its beginning by St John's right elbow, and the centre section above his head. Behind St John is a background of green fruit set in the groins between the ribs.

The most common emblems or attributes associated with St John are a chalice from which a dragon emerges, and a palm. The chalice refers to a legend that a pagan high priest challenged St John to drink from a poisoned cup as a test of his faith. St John survived the test. The dragon symbolises Satan, whom St John overcame. This is a recurring image in medieval art; an example is a roof boss in Norwich Cathedral (CND8).

The palm was given to St John by the Virgin Mary on her deathbed. In nearly all the carvings of the Apocalypse in the south and west walks of the cloisters of Norwich Cathedral, St John, the reputed author of the last book of the Bible, is carved holding a palm.

Here it is probable that in his right hand St John was holding a chalice from which a dragon emerged, and in his left hand a palm.

Boss Number 17 — St James the Great

St James, known as 'the Great', was a son of Zebedee and the elder brother of St John. He was one of the privileged disciples to be present at the Transfiguration and the Agony in the Garden. He was the first of the disciples to suffer martyrdom and was reputed to have travelled to Spain to spread the Gospel. Under Herod Agrippa he was sentenced to death by decapitation. After his death his relics were said to have been taken to Santiago de Compostela.

In this carving he is shown bearded, wearing a heavy brown coat, pleated below the waist, over a grey undergarment which appears at neck-level. A scroll ranges across the upper part of the boss, carrying his name. He is seated on a bench. His right wrist and hand are missing. In his left hand he holds a sword, hilt upward, by the sheath. Across his body is a strap, buckled at the chest, which supports a pilgrim's scrip. St James's attributes include a scallop shell and a sword. It is likely that the saint's right hand held a shell.

Boss Number 19 — St Matthew

St Matthew is bearded, and dressed in a grey gown, tied at the waist. A brown cloak covers his shoulders and the lower part of his body. He holds in his left hand one end of the scroll which unfurls around the boss, framing his head and ending near his right hand. In this hand he holds the middle part of a stout stick, the top half of which probably terminated in the metal head of a halberd. The background is of grey-green fruit.

A number of attributes are associated with St Matthew. As one of the four Evangelists he is often shown holding a scroll, his gospel, with an angel nearby. As a publican, or tax-collector, before he became a disciple, he is seen with a bag of money. But the symbol of his martyrdom is either a sword or a halberd.

A splendid early sixteenth-century carving on a bench-end in St Helen's also depicts the most common symbol of the Evangelist, an angel holding a scroll.

Photograph: Elizabeth Armstrong

Front and back view of the carved bench-end in St Helen's Church depicting St Matthew's angel

Boss Number 20 — St Bartholomew

St Bartholomew has a forked beard and is dressed in a red gown over which is spread in folds a brown cloak. He is seated on a bench with armrests. In the background is an array of red, round fruit. Above the saint's head is a scroll bearing his name, which is threaded through the fruit. His left wrist and hand are missing. In his right hand he carries the triangular fragment of his attribute.

Tradition has it that St Bartholomew was flayed alive at Albanopolis in Armenia. His usual attribute is a flaying knife. In the scene of the Last Supper, carved in the nave vaulting of Norwich Cathedral (NJ10), in a setting in which other disciples display their attributes, one of the disciples, presumed to be St Bartholomew, leans across the table holding a long-bladed knife.

Boss Number 21 — St James the Less

St James is bearded. His head and shoulders are framed by the unfurling scroll which bears his name. Both his gown and cloak are painted brown. What appears to be the grey lining of his cloak lies over his chest and his right arm. His left hand is covered by folds of the cloak. His right hand holds a staff, the top of which has broken off, and the bottom of which is shaped like a hockey-stick. The saint sits on a red bench with armrests.

St James the Less is probably so named to distinguish him from St James the Greater. His attribute is a fuller's club with which he was reputedly beaten to death.

Boss Number 23 — St Matthias

St Matthias is bearded and dressed in a red gown tied at the waist. His brown cloak, falling from his shoulders, has a grey lining. His right hand and wrist have broken off. In his left hand he holds up by its tail a large fish with a glinting eye. The scroll, carrying his name in letters of red and brown, has broken off just above his head.

St Matthias is sometimes depicted with either an axe or a sword as his attribute. It is unusual for him to be represented with a fish as his symbol.

St Matthias after Christ's Ascension was drawn by lot to make up the number of the twelve apostles. He filled the vacancy left by the treachery and death of Judas Iscariot (Acts 1. vv 15-26).

Boss Number 24 — Saint Simon

St Simon's light brown curly hair falls below his ears. He is bearded and dressed in a dark red pleated gown. A brown cloak falls from his shoulders and its grey lining covers the lower part of his gown. He is seated on a red bench with armrests. His left hand and wrist have broken off. He holds a rowing boat in his right hand. The scroll above his head declares his name in dark red letters. In the background is an array of red, round fruit.

St Simon's attribute is usually a book. Both St Jude and St Simon are sometimes represented holding a boat or an oar. In this instance the name on the scroll confirms St Simon's identity.

Boss Number 25 — St Philip

St Philip's head is just below an unbroken scroll that sweeps across the top of the carving. His name appears on the scroll in letters of red and brown. St Philip is bearded and wears a red gown tied at the waist. A brown cloak falls from both shoulders and is draped over his left hand. The cloak's grey-green lining crosses the lower part of his gown. In his right hand he holds a tau cross.

St Philip's attributes are often seen as a sword or a book. Sometimes he is carrying loaves of bread in recognition of his presence at the feeding of the five thousand (John 6. vv 5-7). One legend of St Philip describes his death on a tau cross, and another of his being crucified upside down in the same manner as St Peter.

Boss Number 26 — Anne of Bohemia

The chancel of the original church, which now lies to the east of the present chapel, has a celebrated chestnut ceiling. It comprises 252 panels, on each of which is painted a black eagle with extended wings. At each corner of each panel is a carved boss with a rose-patterned centre surrounded by four foliate designs. This magnificent ceiling is one of the wonders of the church. It is supposed that this great ceiling was inserted by Bishop Henry Despenser, 1369-1406, to commemorate the visit of Richard II and his Queen to St Giles's Hospital in 1383.

Richard II, at the age of fifteen was married in 1382 to Anne of Bohemia, aged sixteen, the eldest daughter of Charles IV, the Holy Roman Emperor. The eagle was the emblem of the Empire (Atherton 413 and Jewson 9).

This carving, reputedly of Anne of Bohemia, is one of four bosses which terminate the vaulting pattern at its end. The head is crowned although the crown is scarcely visible from below. A green veil with a red lining falls over the sides of the queen's face. A high red collar frames her chin and throat. Her hair is held in bunches either side by a caul which is bordered with an alternating pattern of roses and diamonds.

Boss Number 27 — The Angel of St Mark

In drawing up the plan for the subjects of the roof bosses in this chantry chapel vaulting the mason clearly intended that at each cardinal terminal there should be a carving of one of the Evangelists.

In the east is a carving of the Angel of St Mark. The carving is that of a demi-angel. The angel's curling auburn hair is framed by the upward, encircling wings. The angel holds in his two hands a scroll on which the name of the Evangelist is written in Latin. The lion, St Mark's symbol, crouches on the right, with short wavy mane, bright staring eyes, and a red mouth.

The four terminal roof bosses, as each meets the three receiving ribs, serve more the function of a corbel than a keystone.

Photograph: Elizabeth Armstrong

St Mark's lion on a bench-end in St Helen's Church

Boss Number 28 — The Lion

The lion is painted red. In its lying position it turns its head and looks towards the Lion of St Mark in the neighbouring roof boss. Its face is set in a fierce grimace, showing a full set of small lower teeth. Its mane is dark brown and curly. The ill-fitting tail has broken off beneath the lion's buttocks.

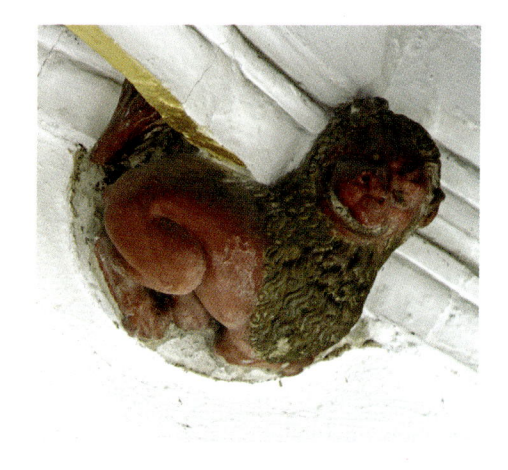

Boss Number 29 — A Hairy Hybrid

The head and shoulders of this creature are those of a woodwose, a wild hairy being whom legend recounted inhabited the woods and the forests. Such creatures can be identified in a variety of medieval art forms. They may be located in the roof bosses (CWA3) and misericords ★(S7) of Norwich Cathedral. However, the rest of the body of the creature carved here is ill-defined, and assumes an animal rather than a human form. A roughly shaped paw or hand on the right is held up to the creature's head.

★ This coding refers to the numbering of the misericords as set out in *Misericords of Norwich Cathedral*, by Martial Rose, Dereham, 2003.

Boss Number 30 — King Henry VI (?)

The head is of a cleric wearing a red skull-cap from which his curly brown hair falls to the level of his ears. The facial features are clearly and finely sculpted. About his neck is a grey-green amice beneath which is a red-rimmed priestly vestment. The effect is impressive and masterly.

There are sound reasons why this carving has previously been taken to be a representation of Henry VI. The central theme of the Coronation of the Virgin has called forth not only the other Four Joys of the Virgin Mary, but also as witnesses to the event the twelve apostles, St Margaret and St Catherine, and the canonised English kings, St Edmund and Edward the Confessor. All are enthroned. If Richard II (Boss Number 34) and his Queen, Anne of Bohemia (Boss Number 26), are also present, then Henry VI and his Queen, Margaret of Anjou, might comprise the matching pair. The two queens face each other on the east-west axis, and the two kings on the south-north axis.

Following the establishment of St Giles's Hospital in the thirteenth century, the two subsequent great building phases took place first in the reign of Richard II and secondly in the reign of the Yorkist kings, Edward IV and Richard III, but that phase was completed in the reign of Henry VII, who had wrested the throne back to the Lancastrian line. The previous Lancastrian king had been Henry VI, who died in 1471.

If this carving represents Henry VI it would be as a compliment to his nephew, the reigning monarch, Henry VII, who intended to move his body from Windsor to the new Lady Chapel he was about to plan for Westminster Abbey. It might also reflect the pious and scholarly nature of Henry VI, who spent a great deal of his life in prayer and meditation, and indeed visited and resided in many of the country's monasteries. He was a devotee at a number of the East Anglian shrines.

Many pilgrims visited his grave at Windsor, and the subsequent miracles of healing associated with such visits were recorded. Although Henry VI was never canonised, at the time that this carving was undertaken his saintliness was widely accepted. In Norfolk there were many influential families, including the Pastons, that were supporters of the House of Lancaster, and within the county there have been found a number of pilgrim badges associated with Henry VI, as well as rood-screen paintings depicting the king, such as that at St Helen's, Gateley, and Binham Abbey.

If this is indeed not a portrayal of King Henry VI but that of a cleric, no one would fill the role better than Bishop Goldwell himself, on whose instructions the work was put in hand and funded, and for whose soul the priests of this chantry chapel were paid to pray.

Boss Number 31 — The Angel of St John

The angel's wings are spread straight along the two groins between the ribs. His auburn hair is handsomely waved, and with his eyes he gazes up towards the central carving of the vaulting. A scroll with letters of red and brown declares that this angel is the symbol of St John. It is not the angel's hands that hold up the scroll but the ivory-coloured talons and beak of an eagle. The eagle's body is painted red and sweeps from left to right across the angel's chest, with its tail extending to the right of the angel's head.

The eagle is the creature associated with St John, as the ox is with St Luke, the lion with St Mark, and the man or angel with St Matthew. These tetramorphic symbols are commonplace in medieval art (Nichols 149-153) and have their origin in Ezekiel 1. vv 5-14 and Revelation 6. vv 1-8. Examples may be seen in Norwich Cathedral carvings in the cloisters (CEB7, CEC7, CED7, CEE7, CSE2, CSE5, CSE8, CSF1).

Boss Number 32 — A Saracen

This seems a strange figure to be found in the company of the Five Joys of the Virgin, the apostles, saints, and kings and queens of England. The face is dark brown, but the lips are painted bright red. And above the top lip is a moustache which droops. The Saracen's hair is very bushy, and on the head is a low turban with a gold band. The red robe has a high collar. The Saracen's right hand is held to his breast; and with the left he clutches a falchion, a slightly curved short sword with a wide blade. The body of the Saracen sweeps to the right, sideways and upwards to meet the lower edge of the rib. This sideways and upwards treatment is common to all the eight carvings in these terminal positions in this vaulting (28, 29, 32, 33, 36, 37, 40, 41).

The features and dress of Saracens can be seen in medieval times on coats of arms, tombstone effigies, misericords, and marginalia of illuminated manuscripts. A Saracen's head, featuring as the crest of a knight's helm, is seen on the alabaster tombs of the Duke of Suffolk in Wingfield, Suffolk, and of Lord Cobham in Lingfield, Surrey. The Saracen or Turkish Knight might also feature in the vernacular drama of the time, in *The N-Town Play*, for instance, as one of the high priest's servants (Play 26), or in the mumming play of St George. Pilgrims visiting the Holy Land were obliged to be escorted and guided by Saracens under the orders of the Mameluke Sultans of Egypt, who controlled Palestine in the latter part of the Middle Ages.

Boss Number 33 — A Gentleman

This figure has previously been described as a benefactor of St Giles's Hospital. It is likely that if a benefactor were to be commemorated in this array of bosses his position might be more prominent than being confined to a terminal corbel. A gentleman is here portrayed with an imposing, tall hat with a red band. From under the hat's brim his hair flares out on both sides. His hair, beard and moustache are auburn. His beard is neatly forked, and he strokes it contentedly with his right hand. His neat, well-fitting green tunic is encircled below the waist by a gold and green girdle. On his right sleeve can be seen five golden buttons. The gentleman has red hose and black shoes. His casual, sideways position is as though he is resting on a couch or on the ground, leaning on his left arm.

Boss Number 34 — Richard II(?)

The sculpting of this head is an accomplished piece of work. The effect is striking, even frightening. A headband, patterned with rosettes, encircles a full head of hair and rests above a furrowed forehead. The side whiskers and moustache are full and flowing, but the beard is short and barely covers the edges of the receiving ribs. The large wide-open eyes are haunted with anxiety.

Is this an image of Richard II, as has been suggested? Perhaps we shall never know for sure. In this patterned vaulting the head is diametrically opposite the head of possibly another king of England, also with no crown, Henry VI. Both kings were indeed *un*crowned; both murdered by usurpers. The rosettes on the headband can be compared to those on the caul of Boss Number 26, which may be a representation of Richard II's queen, Anne of Bohemia.

When Anne of Bohemia died in 1394 Richard II commissioned in the following year effigies of himself and his wife, both uncrowned but wearing headbands, to be placed upon their pre-appointed tomb in Westminster Abbey. These effigies, together with the Westminster panel painting of the king, *c.*1394, the Winchester College stained-glass image of the king and St John the Baptist, *c.*1393, and the Wilton Diptych, *c.*1396, are all considered to be portrait representations of Richard II. In all he is shown as either clean-shaven or with a small wispy beard, but never hirsute as in this St Helen's head.

The Hospital of St Giles had much to be thankful for to Richard II and his queen, and it was as a consequence of their visit in 1383 that a major building campaign on the premises took place under the direction of Henry Despenser, Bishop of Norwich.

It is of course fanciful to theorise about the import of those staring eyes and troubled features, but they convey the apprehension of impending death.

For the Westminster Abbey painting and the Winchester College stained-glass see *Age of Chivalry*, 713, 613.

Boss Number 35 — The Angel of St Luke

The carving of a demi-angel acts as a corbel above the south window. This angel, on the very periphery of the patterned vaulting, looks towards the central boss of the Coronation of the Virgin, tacitly doing homage. The angel has curled hair, a plain tunic, from the back of which spring small feathered wings. In the angel's hands which are delicately carved is a scroll, its middle part broken off. The scroll curls its way round the base of the carving to the right. On this side the muzzle of an ox rests against the scroll. The carving of the ox's face, as that of the angel, is subtly expressive. So much of the painting here, as elsewhere, is analogous to stage make-up painting. Here, for instance, the highlight on the angel's nose tip contrasts with the shading of the upper lip. The whole of the carving is painted in tones of brown.

The carving of the ox denotes the presence of St Luke who with the other three Evangelists, to be seen elsewhere in the vaulting, offers reverence at the Virgin's coronation. The Evangelists with the creatures that represent them are to be seen also in the carvings in the east walk of Norwich Cathedral cloisters (CEB7, St Mark; CEC7, St Matthew; CED7, St Luke; and CEE7, St John).

Photograph: Elizabeth Armstrong

Boss Number 36 — Eleanor of Castile (?)

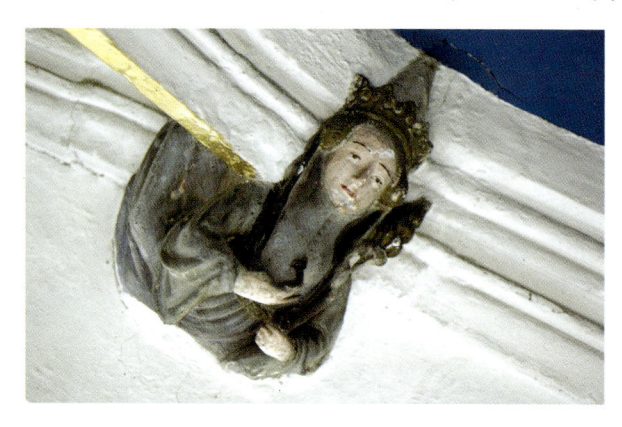

This is a complementary boss to that supposedly of Edward I. It has been thought to represent Eleanor of Castile, the wife of Edward I. Her crown rests on her head-dress, a hennin, a fifteenth century French fashion. The head-dress is in the shape of a tall cone. It was customary for a muslin veil to fall from the very top of the cone. It is possible that such a piece of muslin is depicted either side of the queen's head. One of the bands, falling from her head-dress is terminated with an ornament which she holds in her right hand. It is in the shape of a mouse, the eye of which is clearly visible. The bunches of hair either side are partly covered by a gorget which is buttoned under her chin. Her pleated grey robe is voluminous with wide embroidered sleeves. In her left hand the queen holds a sceptre, described by Cave (54) as a distaff, over her left shoulder. Her decorated girdle is at waist level.

Boss Number 37 — Edward I (?)

The king lies from left to right leaning on his right elbow. From his crown a conical centre-piece, possibly a lion's head, extends to the rib's edge. His hair flows out from either side of his bonnet upon which his crown rests. His eyes look upwards and, unusually for these figures, his mouth is open showing his front teeth. He has side whiskers and a bushy forked beard. His right hand is clenched on his chest, and in his left hand he holds a sceptre over his left shoulder. Over his red tunic, below the waist, is a broad medallioned girdle, decorated with rosettes. His hose are white, and his shoes red.

Edward I (1239-1307) was the son of Henry III and reigned 1272-1307. It was during his reign that the first phase of building St Giles's Hospital would have been completed. This king spent much of his life on the battlefield, in England, Scotland, Wales, as well as crusading abroad, sometimes accompanied by his wife, Eleanor of Castile, whom he married in 1254. On her death in 1290 he gave orders that memorial crosses were to be built at the points of rest as her body was taken from Harby in Nottinghamshire to London.

Boss Number 38 — Margaret of Anjou (?)

The head is carved beneath a curved white ledge. The red head-dress has a green lining. It covers the upper part of the crimped barb which encases the queen's face. This style of barb usually indicates that the wearer is a widow (Gardner 39). Beneath the barb is seen the high collar of a brown dress. The lady's features are smooth and clear and the eyes stare straight ahead.

Margaret of Anjou (1430-1482) was queen to Henry VI. She led the Lancastrian forces in some of the engagements in the Wars of the Roses. She was imprisoned after her side's defeat at Tewkesbury in 1471 by Edward IV. Her husband was murdered soon afterwards. On her release in 1476 she returned to France where she died a few years later.

Walter Lyhart, Bishop of Norwich, 1446-1472, who commissioned the building of the cloisters at St Giles's Hospital, had been confessor to Margaret of Anjou. In 1449 he had entertained Henry VI in his episcopal palace in Norwich (Goulburn 473). The carving of this roof boss would have been almost contemporary with the time of Queen Margaret's death.

Boss Number 39 — The Angel of St Matthew

Unlike the other bosses in the vaulting this one is extensively damaged. The angel's wings, upper face, and the area beneath the chin are mutilated. The changes are more likely to have been caused by masonry repairs rather than by deliberate vandalism. The angel's nostrils have not been carved but are delineated with lines of black paint. The three other angels at the terminal cardinal points of the vaulting are carved with the symbols of the Evangelists, St John, St Mark, and St Luke. It would therefore seem most probable that this carving represents the Angel of St Matthew. The symbol for St Matthew is a winged man or angel.

Boss Number 40 — A Physician

This is a cruder carving of a physician with a urine flask than that of Boss Number 41. He is dressed in a red tunic. At his neck is a dark brown tippet. He has white hose and brown shoes. He holds up the urine flask near his head, perhaps to examine its contents.

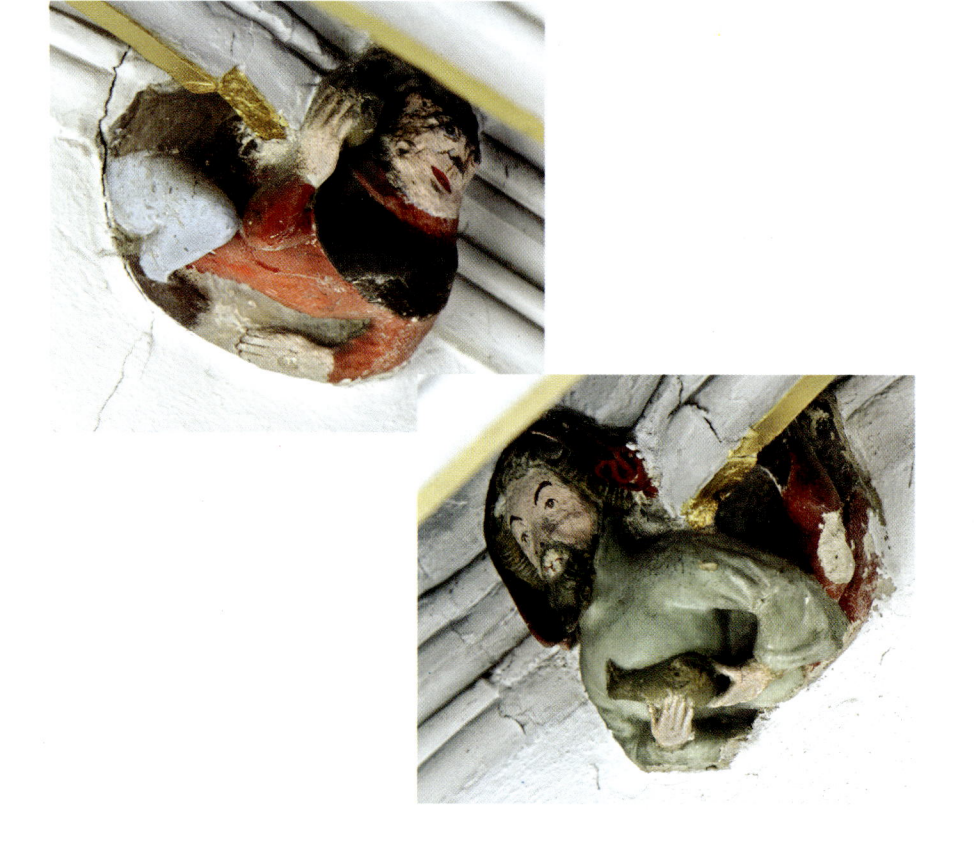

Boss Number 41 — A Physician

The carving shows a man wearing a red head-dress the folds of which fall over his shoulders. He is bearded and his mouth is open, showing upper and lower teeth. His green tunic has golden wristbands and a gold armband above his left elbow. He wears red hose and black shoes. In his hands he holds a urine flask.

The age-old practice of examining a patient's water was even more a critical aid in diagnosis of the state of a patient's health in the Middle Ages than now. St Giles's Hospital would have welcomed a visiting physician to attend the sick, but its primary concern for its inmates was that they should make their confession, attend services, and prepare their souls for the hereafter.

References

Alexander, J., and Binski, P., *Age of Chivalry*, London, 1987

Atherton, I. et al. (ed) *Norwich Cathedral: Church, City and Diocese 1096-1996*, London, 1996

Binski, P., *A Guide to the Thornham Parva Retable*, London, 2004

Binski, P.& Panayotova, S.(eds.), *The Cambridge Illuminations*, London, 2005

Cave, C. J. P., *Roof Bosses in Medieval Churches*, Cambridge, 1948

Cheetham, F., *Medieval English Alabasters*, Oxford, 1984

Cautley, H. M., *Norfolk Churches*, Ipswich, 1949

Duffy, E., *The Stripping of the Altars*, Yale, 1992

Gardner, A., *Alabaster Tombs*, Cambridge, 1940

Gordon, D. et. al., *The Wilton Diptych*, London, 1993

Goulburn, E. M. and Symonds, H., *On the Ancient Sculptures in the Roof of Norwich Cathedral*, London, 1876

Hassall, W. O. (ed), *Facsimile of The Holkham Bible Picture Book*, London, 1954

Hedgecoe, J., & Rose, M., *Norwich Cathedral Roof Bosses*, CD-ROM, Norwich, 2001

Jewson, C. B., *History of the Great Hospital, Norwich*, Norwich, 1980

Mâle, E., *The Gothic Image*, London, 1972

Marks, R., & Williamson, P. (eds), *Gothic Art for England 1400-1547*, London, 2003

Marks, R., *Image and Devotion in Late Medieval England*, Stroud, 2004

Nichols, A. E., *The Early Art of Norfolk*, Kalamazoo, 2002

Norton, C., Park, D., Binski, P., *Dominican Painting in East Anglia, The Thornham Parva Retable and the Musée de Cluny Frontal*, Woodbridge, 1987

Pevsner, N., *North-East Norfolk and Norwich*, London, 1988

Rawcliffe, C., *The Hospitals of Medieval Norwich*, Norwich, 1995

Rawcliffe, C., *Medicine for the Soul*, Bodmin, 1999

Rawcliffe, C., and Wilson, R. (eds), *Medieval Norwich*, London, 2004

Rose, M., *The Misericords of Norwich Cathedral*, Dereham, 2003

Rubin, M., *The Hollow Crown*, London, 2005

Spector, S. (ed), *The N-Town Play*, Oxford, 1991

Tatton-Brown, T., and Mortimer, R. (eds.), *Westminster Abbey: the Lady Chapel of Henry VII*, Woodbridge, 2003

Tristram, E. W., *The Erpingham Gate* (Ninth Annual Report of Friends of Norwich Cathedral, Norwich, 1938)